First World War
and Army of Occupation
War Diary
France, Belgium and Germany

19 DIVISION
Divisional Troops
86 Brigade Royal Field Artillery
15 July 1915 - 30 December 1916

WO95/2067/3

The Naval & Military Press Ltd
www.nmarchive.com
Published in association with The National Archives

Published by

The Naval & Military Press Ltd

Unit 10 Ridgewood Industrial Park,

Uckfield, East Sussex,

TN22 5QE England

Tel: +44 (0) 1825 749494

www.naval-military-press.com

www.nmarchive.com

This diary has been reprinted in facsimile from the original. Any imperfections are inevitably reproduced and the quality may fall short of modern type and cartographic standards.

© **Crown Copyright**
Images reproduced by permission of The National Archives, London, England, 2015.

Contents

Document type	Place/Title	Date From	Date To
Heading	WO95/2067 19 Div-86 Bde RFA July 1915-Dec 1916		
Heading	19th Division 86th Brigade R.F.A. Jly 1915-1916 Dec.		
Heading	19th Division 86th Bde. R.F.A. Vol I July to Oct 15		
War Diary	Bulford	15/07/1915	15/07/1915
War Diary	Southampton Water	16/07/1915	17/07/1915
War Diary	Havre	18/07/1915	18/07/1915
War Diary	Audriques	19/07/1915	19/07/1915
War Diary	Polincove	19/07/1915	23/07/1915
War Diary	Wallon-Cappel	24/07/1915	24/07/1915
War Diary	Harte-Vent	30/07/1915	30/07/1915
War Diary	Cordescure	07/08/1915	24/08/1915
War Diary	Le Touret	24/08/1915	02/10/1915
Heading	19th Division 86th Bde. R.F.A. Vol. 2 Oct 15		
War Diary	Le Plantin	02/10/1915	03/10/1915
War Diary	Le Touret	03/10/1915	05/11/1915
Heading	19th Division 86th Bde: R.F.A. Vol:3 Nov 15		
War Diary	Le Touret	06/11/1915	23/11/1915
War Diary	St Venant	24/11/1915	30/11/1915
Heading	19th Div 86th Bde: R.F.A. Vol: 4 Dec 1915		
War Diary	St Venant	03/12/1915	03/12/1915
War Diary	Vielle Chappelle	04/12/1915	31/12/1915
Heading	19th D 86th Bde: R.F.A. Vol 5 Jan 16		
War Diary	Vielle Chapelle	01/01/1916	31/01/1916
Heading	86th Bde. R.F.A. 19 Vol 6		
War Diary	St Venant	01/02/1916	16/02/1916
War Diary	Bout Deville	16/02/1916	29/02/1916
War Diary	St Venant	01/02/1916	20/02/1916
War Diary	Bout Deville	21/02/1916	29/02/1916
Heading	86 R F A Vol 7		
War Diary	Bout Deville	01/03/1916	31/03/1916
War Diary	Bout Deville	01/04/1916	30/04/1916
Heading	D.H.G. 3rd Echelon, The Base Herewith War Diary of 86th Brigade R.F.A. for months of May 1916, and June 1916	02/07/1916	02/07/1916
War Diary	Therouanne	01/05/1916	09/05/1916
War Diary	Yzeux	14/05/1916	30/06/1916
Heading	Headquarters 86th Brigade R.F.A. July 1916		
War Diary	Albert	01/07/1916	31/07/1916
War Diary	Albert	20/07/1916	31/07/1916
Heading	19th Divisional Artillery. 86th Brigade Royal Field Artillery August 1916		
War Diary	Albert	01/08/1916	13/08/1916
War Diary	Dranoutre	14/08/1916	31/08/1916
Heading	War Diary of 86th Brigade R.F.A. from 1.9.16 to 30.9.16 (Volume XV)		
War Diary	Dranoutre	01/09/1916	11/09/1916
War Diary	Neuve Eglise	11/09/1916	30/09/1916
Heading	War Diary Of 86th Bde R.F.A. From 1st Oct to 31st Oct 1916		
War Diary	Neuve Eglise	01/10/1916	02/10/1916

War Diary	Meteren	03/10/1916	03/10/1916
War Diary	Fletre	04/10/1916	05/10/1916
War Diary	Vauchelles	06/10/1916	07/10/1916
War Diary	Coigneux	08/10/1916	09/10/1916
War Diary	Hebuterne	10/10/1916	17/10/1916
War Diary	Albert	18/10/1916	31/10/1916
War Diary	Albert	01/11/1916	14/11/1916
War Diary	Nr Albert	15/11/1916	30/11/1916
War Diary	Nr Albert	01/12/1916	30/12/1916

WO95/2067

19 Div - 86 Bde

RFA

Jul 1915 - Dec 1916

19TH DIVISION

86TH BRIGADE R.F.A.
JLY. 1915 - ~~MAY 1917~~
1916 DEC

Became Army Field Artillery
Brigade
4 Army

121/
7517

19th Division

86th Bde: R.F.A.
Vol I
July to Oct 15.

Nov '17

Army Form C. 2118

Page 1

86th Brigade R.F.A.
19th Division

WAR DIARY or INTELLIGENCE SUMMARY
(Erase heading not required.)

Instructions regarding War Diaries and Intelligence Summaries are contained in F.S. Regs, Part II. and the Staff Manual respectively. Title Pages will be prepared in manuscript.

Place	Date 1915	Hour	Summary of Events and Information	Remarks and references to Appendices
Bulford	15th July	midnight	Brigade left Bulford & entrained at Amesbury for Southampton docks.	
Southampton Water	16th "	4 p.m.	Entrained on transport "City of Dunkirk". Lay at anchor in Southampton Water till following day	
	17th July	2.30 p.m.	Weighed anchor from Southampton Water	
HAVRE	16th July	1.0 a.m.	Arrived at HAVRE	
	16th July	6 p.m.	Entrained at Gare des marchandises, Havre at 9.30 p.m.	
AUDRUIQUES	19th July	5.30 p.m.	Arrived at AUDRUIQUES, marching from there to billets at POLINCOVE	
POLINCOVE	19-25	9.0 a.m.	Left POLINCOVE for WALLON CAPPEL arriving there at 3 p.m.	
WALLON-CAPPEL	24th	6.30 p.m.	Left for ST VENANT arriving there at noon, camping at HARTE-VENT	
HARTE-VENT	30th	9 a.m.	Marched to CORDESCURE near the Bois d'AVAL, district of MERVILLE	
CORDESCURE	August 7th	9.30 p.m.	Inspected by General Sir James Willcocks	
"	24th	2.30 p.m.	Marched to LE TOURET & on the night of the 24th occupied gun positions of the 35th Bde. The batteries remained under the Tactical command of Col. Oliphant until the 31st Augt.	
LE TOURET	Aug "			
LE TOURET	31st	10 a.m.	A grouping of the Brigades took place and became known as Indian I & Indian II. The former under command of Lt Col. A.S. Wilson D.S.O. comprised 87th RFA Brigade & the B/87 and Batteries A/86; C/86; The front covered by the group extended from A/86 & C/86. Southern limit of front to S 27 & 9.3. with A/89 on right followed by C/87, B/89 A/87 & C/86. Covery APB.FC. sections of the 58th Infantry Brigade.	
	Sept 5th 19th		Orders for regrouping (to be prepared for) were issued.	
	20th	7 a.m.	Regrouping of the groups of artillery were as follows; Bethune A/86 B/86, A/87, B/87 A/89 B/89 — Trench with the How 4.5 A/89. The enemy front line much	Signature A9G 1.9 — Rhenvalle Infantry sections & both sections A7B.

1875 Wt. W593/826 1,000,000 4/15 J.B.C. & A. A.D.S.S./Forms/C.2118.

Army Form C. 2118

Page (2)

WAR DIARY
or
INTELLIGENCE SUMMARY
(Erase heading not required.)

Place	Date 1915 Sept.	Hour	Summary of Events and Information	Remarks and references to Appendices
LE TOURET	20th		Inspection section & situation won by 9th Welch Reg. & 9 R.W. Fusiliers under Brig. Gen. Stuart.	
	21st	8 am	Bombardment of enemies trenches commenced between the points A3a11 – A3a84, whilst there was Hr allotted some gas attack, were bombarded with H.E. by the 18 pdr battery & 4.5 How. Bty.	
		2 pm	18 pdr battery opened fire on enemys front line wire entanglements.	
		8 pm	B/85 – D/87 fired two 6" gun salvoes at broken intervals. Every three hrs the right on general targets. The remainder of the 18 pdr battery fired 2 gun salvoes during the night on enemy trenches.	
	22nd		Bombardment continues. The enemy showed but little activity in op 8.	
	23rd		Bombardment continues. The enemy were active in shelling C/87 which had moved into a new position with the open in the 1.95	
	24th	2 pm	moved in its Forward Report centre at A1.C.88 with the Brigadier General 7/R 58th Inf.	
	25	5.50	Assault with little fierce under heavy artillery bombardment. The morning was damp with the wind most favourable from S.S.W. The enemy met with heavy tanks from his machine guns artillery and infantry, & moreover the machine 15 front line trenches were commanded by the artillery until some of the infantry had reached with 90 yards of them. The fire was then lifted of the second line, and enemy communication trenches with the copse & shelling houses & of the Estates & Popes Nose. all this heavy bombardment gun retalk.	

1875. Wt. W593/326 1,000,000 4/15 J.B.C. & A. A.D.S.S./Forms/C. 2118.

Army Form C. 2118
(3)

WAR DIARY
or
INTELLIGENCE SUMMARY
(Erase heading not required.)

Place	Date 1915	Hour	Summary of Events and Information	Remarks and references to Appendices
	26th	10 a.m.	The fighting ceased & those of our infantry who were able had regained the cover of their own trenches. The shelling of our front line trenches by the enemy has very heavy & a large number of heavy shells burst in the front line trenches, causing many casualties. During the remainder of the day nothing took place of an important nature.	
		8 p.m.	The battns were ordered to cover the front line trenches in order to on the shower. The enemy artillery with the stretcher bearers gather the wounded. Enemy were fairly active, shells, support trenches at various times of the day. Orders were received that the groups was not to fire except more 48 hrs or 4½ ammunition unless an attack came on by the enemy. Shelling by the enemy of support trenches in Festubert at various times.	
	27th		Shelling by the Enemy of the areas around Festubert & Le Plantin & Ertainnes. occurred a few causalities amongst- troops occurred. Our artillery was not replying.	FESTUBERT · LE PLANTIN
	28th		Intermittent shelling by the Enemy around Festubert, Le Plantin & Rue d'EPINETTE.	
	29th		A number of the Enemy shells did not explode.	
	30th		Arrangements being made for relief of 58th Infantry Brigade by 59th Inf Bde.	
	31st Oct Sept		Enemy seem to have knowledge of reliefs as shelling becomes more prevalent. 57th Infantry Brigade relieves 58th Infantry Brigade & become portion of and occupies the Central Zone, from ORKNEY ROAD to PIPE TRENCH	
	2			

121/7517

19th Nivain

St M Rae: RSA.
Vol 8 2
Oct 15

Army Form C. 2118

WAR DIARY or INTELLIGENCE SUMMARY
(Erase heading not required.)

86. F.A Brigade

Instructions regarding War Diaries and Intelligence Summaries are contained in F.S. Regs., Part II. and the Staff Manual respectively. Title Pages will be prepared in manuscript.

Place	Date 1915	Hour	Summary of Events and Information	Remarks and references to Appendices
LE PLANTIN	Oct 2		Covering the 57th Infantry Brigade, Indian Lt is taken over by 15 Meerut Division R.A; 87th F.A 4 reserve and III Group H.Q returns to LE TOURET	
LE TOURET	3	10 am	Indian II R.A Group becomes Indian III R.A group & comprises all batteries of the 86 & R.A Brigade A/89 Howitzer with two batteries of 87th F.A Brigade in reserve. The enemy were quiet along the Front during the day. Shelling of the Rue du Bois with 5.9 caused several casualties in one of the batteries of the 86 F.A.B grade.	
	4		H.Q. Div Art. permit use of ammunition for retaliation & registration & rus Jones. Enemy is keeping more active. So passed during the night.	
	5		Retaliation for shelling on R.A.B. had temporal results. Enemy Smiled. H.q. Div Art have granted permission to expend 100 rounds on present targets, in conjunction with infantry.	
	6		The enemy were quiet throughout the night & day. A conference of officers was held in Group H.Q & arrangements made for a special strafe of the ORCHARD in conjunction with the Infantry & machine gun stations.	
	7	4 pm	An effective bombardment of the Enemys front & Communication trenches was carried out by the R.A. group, machine guns & Infantry, co-operating. The enemy did not show any keen retaliation by Artillery + now & Gun.	
	8		Retaliation on both sides both places every the day. The enemy shelling the support trench & entrance & Communication trenches at Indian VILLAGE. TUBE STATION - FESTUBERT	
	9		There is nothing of importance to report. The enemy retaliation has been silent by Artillery.	
	10		The day has been quiet along the Front.	
	11		During the night the enemy was active bombing the ORCHARD. The Group R.A. carried out	

1875 Wt. W593/826 1,000,000 4/15 J.B.C. & A. A.D.S.S./Forms/C. 2118.

Army Form C. 2118

86 F.A. Bde (B)

WAR DIARY
or
INTELLIGENCE SUMMARY
(Erase heading not required.)

Instructions regarding War Diaries and Intelligence Summaries are contained in F.S. Regs., Part II and the Staff Manual respectively. Title Pages will be prepared in manuscript.

Place	Date 1915	Hour	Summary of Events and Information	Remarks and references to Appendices
~~Le Pretoral~~ LE TOURET	Oct. 11		Carried out a systematic retaliation which was effective, & silenced the bombing.	
	12		Usual artillery retaliation has taken place. The enemy placed a 5.9 into the position of E/86 R.A. wounding four men.	
	13		Nothing of importance has taken place on the Group front. The usual retaliation of artillery.	
	14	1–2 pm	An organized co-operative shoot took place on the Turnips front supported [Compression] trench – in the vicinity of the ORCHARD. The enemy did not retaliate.	
	15		Nothing of importance has taken place. The usual desultory retaliation. Weather misty.	
	16		The weather has become very misty. Observation impossible. A few previous up from our own shell fires yesterday proves to be of Frost origin.	
	17		Weather still foggy preventing any observation.	
	18		The enemy snipers have been exceedingly active, and fog wire active with transports on the Rue du MARAIS. Our artillery engaged them & prevented any further operations.	
	19		Weather still misty – the front is exceptionally quiet. Intermittent retaliation with fair — during the afternoon.	
	20		The enemy seen to have taken advantage of the fog to establish snipers posts. These have become very active when located they have been disposed of by Stokesfield fire. A hostile battery was located & shelled at A.4 a 5½.9, with satisfactory results.	
	21	10 am	Indian II R.A. Group became known III R.A. group. T. Company the 86 R.A. Brigade, 27/69 field battery, a counter battery, r 89/69 A.A. Howitzer battery. The group were supporting	

Army Form C. 2118

WAR DIARY
or
INTELLIGENCE SUMMARY

86. F.A. Brigade (6)

(Erase heading not required.)

Instructions regarding War Diaries and Intelligence Summaries are contained in F.S. Regs., Part II. and the Staff Manual respectively. Title Pages will be prepared in manuscript.

Place	Date 1915	Hour	Summary of Events and Information	Remarks and references to Appendices
~~Estaires~~ LE TOURET	Oct 21	10 am	will support the 56th Infantry Brigade, from ORKNEY ROAD communication trench to PIPE Communication trench inclusive. R.A. Group Commander Lt.Col. H.S. Wilson. The enemy was active with bombs on its orchard salient. to which the artillery replied with effect. Traffic along the Rue du Marais was active, another group of Fug.	
	22		The enemy have constructed a strong machine gun redoubt. close to the front line trench near the orchard salient. This has replied by ten rounds by 15 18 pdr without any satisfactory distinctive result.	
	23	2 pm.	The enemy carried out some retaliation by 16"and of Aeroplane observation on the Rue du Bois no damage was done. The group artillery replies daily.	
	24		The weather has again become less mild for observation. The front has been very quiet.	
	25"		Weather mild, slight retaliation, observation impossible. Saving reported the hostile enemy front line trench. Traffic along the Rue du Marais was dispersed by Group artillery fire.	
	26		Battery positions group rearranged for special replacing on the enemy's front line trench C/89 thoroughly bullets within the groups of Indian II ore section commenced action tonight.	
	27	12 noon 3 pm. 6 pm.	Enemy artillery was very active shelling Rue de Epinette - Indian Village - Orchard - A hostile Biplane flew over but was over the orchard actively	

1875 WT W593/826 1,000,000 6/15 JB.C&A. A.D.S.S./Forms/C. 2118.

Army Form C. 2118

WAR DIARY
or
INTELLIGENCE SUMMARY
(Erase heading not required.)

S6 F.A. Brigade (7)

Instructions regarding War Diaries and Intelligence Summaries are contained in F. S. Regs., Part II. and the Staff Manual respectively. Title Pages will be prepared in manuscript.

Place	Date 1915	Hour	Summary of Events and Information	Remarks and references to Appendices
Le Plantin	Oct 28	12.45 pm	The Enemy was quiet with their artillery; the Howitzer batty bombarded LORGIES	
LE TOURET	29		Rain & most prevent observation. Some tunnel retaliation was carried out at the names of the Infantry.	
	30	12.15	Bombardment of the redoubt known as the "Cupola" was carried out, also a bombardment of the Enemy billets in BEAU PUITS and LORGIES — the Enemy made but a weak reply.	
	31		Enemy were very active with artillery fire but down the morning & afternoon;- The Battery zones of A/K6 & B/K6 have been changed to suit the convenience of T Battery R.H.A. which has taken a position on the ground in front.	
	Nov 1		Retaliation to the Enemy fire at the request of the Infantry. The weather owing to the wet weather are in a very desperate condition.	
	2		The Enemy were active shelling the Rue de l'Epinette – INDIAN VILLAGE – and our reserve trenches. Our artillery replied in retaliation	
	3		The Enemy repeated the shelling of yesterday.	
	4		There was very slight activity on either side, the weather being wet & cold	
	5		Retaliation at the request of the Infantry – for Enemy bombing.	

1875 Wt. W593/826 1,000,000 4/15 J.B.C. & A. A.D.S.S./Forms/C.2118.

86th Bde: R.F.A.
Vol: 3

121/7795.

19th Division

Nov 15.

Army Form C. 2118

WAR DIARY
or
INTELLIGENCE SUMMARY

(Erase heading not required.)

86th Brigade

Place	Date 1915	Hour	Summary of Events and Information	Remarks and references to Appendices
~~Le Touret~~ Le Touret	6		Enemy Artillery fired motars even very active all day. SHETLAND ROAD Communication trench suffering in consequence. Our artillery replied. It is noticed that our retaliation so invariably doubled that of the enemy in response.	
	7		Both day & night have been exceptionally quiet, weather wet & cold.	
	8		Weather wet & cold. Shelling by the enemy not much worse. Retaliation on the front line by our artillery.	
	9		Enemy artillery more active than usual. Shelling never twelve will shrapnel the S.	
	10		An organised strafe of the enemy's front line from S.22.c.1.7 – S.22.c.3.5 was carried out by the 16th. bn. battery, with very satisfactory results. The enemy replied with a bombardment of PRINCES ROAD – CHOCOLATE CORNER – and support trenches near TUBE STATION	
	11		The weather in the early morning was misty – but towards 11 am cleared sufficiently to permit observation. The enemy were persistent in their bombing of the trenches at SHETLAND ROAD	
	12		A few emplacements has been located at S.22.d.4.5. This shift was engaged by B/86. Enemy fired on our communication trenches at various times with 77.m.m.	

Signed Ashton Alcock
ADJUTANT, 86TH T.F.A.

Army Form C. 2118

WAR DIARY
or
INTELLIGENCE SUMMARY
(Erase heading not required.)

86th F.A. Bde (9)

Place	Date	Hour	Summary of Events and Information	Remarks and references to Appendices
LE TOURET	1915 Nov 13		Hostile artillery was quiet during the day. Cooking parts was seen at S.22.c.5.8. and dispersed by 9/82.	
	14		Enemy shelled Princes Road and Rue d'L. Epinette at frequent intervals during the day, retaliation by our artillery has been effective.	
	15		Weather conditions for observation have been Indifferent. Considerable damage has been done to Enemy O.P.'s along our front.	
	16		Continued retaliation to F.A.? Group 18 pdrs Exploded 3 Minenwerfer and most damage has been an Enemy fire trench at S.22.c.3½.5½ and most damage has been done to his parapets and Communication Trenches. Enemy trench mortars have been active on Orchard Salient. Each round was repaid with interest by 18 pdr covering that portion of the front.	
	17		A bombardment was carried out by the Heavy batteries in Conjunction with the 18 pdrs of this Front, on the Lawins Enemy retaliated on our front line following the bombardment but with little effect.	
	18		At rare intervals fire was directed on Violaines to prevent repairs to works damaged by to bombards burst of yesterday.	
	19		Weather throughout the day has been fair for observation. Enemy artillery was inactive.	
	20		Continued Artillery demonstration took place on Enemy front line trench from S.22.c.11½.7. to S.22.c.5.4. The 2 Howrs Engaged Continued firing 8" Hows, 4.5 Hows, and 18 pdrs of this Front, considerable damage was done. Answer that struck the Enemy were parties of material being thrown in the air.	

J.P. Thomas Lieut, R.F.A.
ADJUTANT, 86th BRIGADE R.F.A.

Army Form C. 2118

WAR DIARY
or
INTELLIGENCE SUMMARY
(Erase heading not required.)

86th FA Bde (O)

Place	Date	Hour	Summary of Events and Information	Remarks and references to Appendices
LE TOURET	Nov 1915 22/23		The 86th Brigade has relieved in its position of the line by the 7th and 46th Divisional Artillery, and took up billets in the St Venant - Berguette Road, near St Venant	
ST VENANT	24 to 30		Brigade in reserve. Motion and battery training.	

(signature) LIEUT. R.F.A.
ADJUTANT, 86TH BRIGADE R.F.A.

86th Bde: R.F.A.
Vol. 4

7910/121

19th Bgi

Dec 1915

Army Form C. 2118

WAR DIARY
or
INTELLIGENCE SUMMARY

86th Brigade RFA (1)

(Erase heading not required.)

Instructions regarding War Diaries and Intelligence Summaries are contained in F.S. Regs., Part II. and the Staff Manual respectively. Title Pages will be prepared in manuscript.

Place	Date	Hour	Summary of Events and Information	Remarks and references to Appendices
St Venant	DEC 1915 1		Brigade in reserve –	
	3		B Battery, D Battery, and 1 section of C Battery 86th Brigade moved into action in relief of the 46th Divisional Artillery – A Battery and the remaining section of C Battery 86th Brigade RFA marched to Vielle Chapelle and remained in reserve.	
Vielle Chapelle H	5		B/86 was in support with the Right Artillery Group, together with one gun each from C and D Batteries. 86th Brigade RFA which act as Flank Reinforcement. The remaining 3 guns of D/86 and 1 gun of C/86 act as Flank Reinforcement guns for the Left artillery group. The 86th Brigade Ammunition Column moved from St Venant to its billets at Zelobes.	
	6		Enemy artillery has active throughout the day, principally smaller calibre. A divisional artillery scheme was carried out, fire being directed on the enemy front line at the Bones Head. 5'16 a.5.7'12 and Communication trenches in rear. Available damage was done to his parapets.	
	7		The Enemy has been to be repairing his parapets at 5'16 a.5'3'7 and has defences by B/86.	
	8		A bombardment of the Enemy's trenches at S.S.a.2.3. arranged for to-day was only partially carried out as the weather condition made artillery observation impossible	

J. G. Colon Lieut. R.F.A.
ADJUTANT, 86th BRIGADE R.F.A.

Army Form C. 2118

WAR DIARY
or
INTELLIGENCE SUMMARY

86th Brigade (12)

(Erase heading not required.)

Instructions regarding War Diaries and Intelligence Summaries are contained in F.S. Regs., Part II. and the Staff Manual respectively. Title Pages will be prepared in manuscript.

Place	Date	Hour	Summary of Events and Information	Remarks and references to Appendices
Neuve Chapelle	Dec 1915 9		Enemy artillery reply to our shelling of their front line at S16.c.6.10 was light.	
	10		Much damage has been done to the enemy's wire at S.S.d. 2.3 and his parapets here badly knocked about.	
	11		He has directed on the enemy Communication Trench at S.22.C.8.6. He immediately retaliated on the Brewery S.P. and front line.	
	12		A combined offensive operation took place on the enemy front line at S.S.b.9.8 and selected points in his Communication Trenches — during the night he was prevented from hindering repairs by fire from 6 to 7.8 p.m.	
	13		Hostile artillery was active during the day, a divisional artillery scheme was carried out on the enemy Back Area trenches 5 to 9.1 to S.16.a.9.4. No movement of the enemy was observed during the bombardment.	
	14		The night from 7 bombarded the enemy front line trenches at S.16.a.6.4 to S.16.d.3.6. Several Carl Japs were made and a considerable width of trench was blown in the air.	
	15		A Combined Stafe of heaven and 18 phers took place on the Green known at the Ferme Cour St Avene, considerable damage was done, the enemy retaliated with Field Guns on our front line at S.S.C.	
	16		Enemy artillery has unusually quiet all day, the 18 phers were employed in harassing the enemy infantry reliefs during the night.	

J.G. Johns / LIEUT, R.E.N
ADJUTANT, 86th BRIGADE R.F.A.

WAR DIARY
or
INTELLIGENCE SUMMARY 8th A Bde

Army Form C. 2118

Place	Date 1915	Hour	Summary of Events and Information	Remarks and references to Appendices
Neuve Chapelle	Dec 17		The light was much too bad to-day to do accurate shooting for effect. Enemy retaliation was weak	
	18		Very foggy, all day observation was impossible	
	19		Enemy shelled Battalion Headquarters at Rue du Bois and Trench Communications 5. 9 hows. Retaliation was shown by them on our camp during the morning.	
	20		Wire cutting was carried out at point S.10.c.8.1, and the enemy front line and communication trenches received attention from the 18 pdrs of both groups.	
	21		The light has been bad for observation during the whole day. The enemy was evidently annoyed by our cutting his wire, as he retaliated here than usual.	
	22		Wire cutting was again carried out by the 18 pdrs with considerable effect	
	23		Enemy artillery has been more active than usual. Particularly his field guns, a good lot of light shell was carried out and their line seemed to be generally found to be any prolonged retaliation than we have so far received since we came into action in this group.	
	24		A group of about 100 place or LORGIES and many knots have been noted by aircraft the houses, at night the wire was directed on LA TOURELLE Cross Roads to catch infantry reliefs	

J.P. Shore /LIEUT. R.F.A.
ADJUTANT, 8th BRIG. R.F.A.

Army Form C. 2118

WAR DIARY
or
INTELLIGENCE SUMMARY 86th Bde
(Erase heading not required.)

Instructions regarding War Diaries and Intelligence Summaries are contained in F.S. Regs., Part II. and the Staff Manual respectively. Title Pages will be prepared in manuscript.

Place	Date 1915	Hour	Summary of Events and Information	Remarks and references to Appendices
VIELLE CHAPELLE	Dec 25		The Enemy shelled systematically every half hour with 77 m.m. on Rue de Bois and Princes Road from 5pm to 8pm this was in retaliation for our fire on the communication trenches La Tourelle and vicinity	
	26		Hostile artillery not so active as usual to-day, working parties were fired at S16.d.7.7. and dispersion by our fire. One section of 86 moved into action for some artillery operations under the direction of the light group. Enemy shells Richburg Church with fair effect.	
	27		The line was effectively cut at S.16.a.5/7.8 and the Expenditure of 195 rounds has well spent. The section of 86 returned to its reserve billets.	
	28		Enemy artillery has particularly active to-day principally on the Rue de Bois	
	29		Working parties were fired on and also places in the Enemy front line which had been repaired lately received attention.	
	30		Climatic conditions have been bad for observation to-day	
	31		Hostile artillery was active throughout the day and our own batteries than usual were noticed – working parties at S.S.5.a.5.4 were dispersed.	

Gpohone? LIEUT. R.F.A.
ADJUTANT, 86TH F BdE R.F.A.

1875. Wt. W593/826 1,000,000 4/15 J.B.C. & A. A.D.S.S./Forms/C. 2118.

86th Bde. R.F.A.
Vol. 5
Jan. 16

15th D

WAR DIARY or INTELLIGENCE SUMMARY

Army Form C. 2118

8th Brigade RFA

Place	Date 1916 Jan	Hour	Summary of Events and Information	Remarks and references to Appendices
VIEILLE CHAPELLE	1		Good results have been obtained from the fire of the Right Group Artillery on houses at S.28.b.2.6. - Sixtienne and Wooden Buildings E of same shown a front scheme was carried out on TOULOTTE, COUR D'AVOUE AND MOULIN D'EAU, the third phase was Cancelled owing to bad climatic conditions for observation.	
	2			
	3		Enemy artillery was fairly active to-day, light was good for observation but no movement was noticed in the German lines	
	4		Line was directed a protector billets in rear of the enemy lines and a considerable amount of damage was done	
	5		Front scheme was carried out on houses near S.22.a.4.y. S.22.b.6.4. both hours and 18 pdrs making a burst of direct hits. The Enemy retaliated on CHOCOLATE CORNER and PRINCES ROAD but with little effect.	
	6	-	Enemy 97 mm batteries were an active to-day also his machine guns.	
	7	.	C/8L sul laie at S.16.a.7 9½ for the Right front 2½ Rending 199 rounds with good effect.	
	8	.	Hostile artillery was active especially on Chateau Redoubt and frequently in the Vicinity of Neuve Chapelle. A retaliation for our own cutting operations	

WAR DIARY
or
INTELLIGENCE SUMMARY
(Erase heading not required.)

86th Brigade RFA   Army Form C. 2118

Place	Date 1916 Jan	Hour	Summary of Events and Information	Remarks and references to Appendices
VIELLE CHAPELLE	9		From 11.15 a.m. to 4.15 p.m. the Enemy's 8" and 5.9's shelled LACOUTURE. Every three minutes 3 direct hits were made on the East end of the Church. A fair amount of damage was done to houses near the Church.	
	10		Climatic conditions for observation were very poor to-day. Heavy artillery fired on Rebelsring during the afternoon, a hostile aeroplane was observing for them.	
	11		A Divisional Scheme was carried out on Enemy's front and support trenches at S16 c.8.1 to S16 a 6.8½ to S16 a 6.8½. No enemy movement was noticeable.	
	12		Enemy artillery was unusually quiet during most of the day. A/86 spent 71 rounds with good effect on 2nd line trench at S.S.6 C.7.7. and moved traps in ditches at S.S.6 C.9.7. to 10 p.m.	
	13		Fire at S.S. 6.9.8½ was noticed to have been retained and was reported by A/86. Enemy artillery was again very passive.	
	14		A 77 m.m. battery was located at T.19. C.3.4. The latter was firing salvos at the SAVOY CP during the morning.	
	15		Enemy artillery more active than usual during day. Operations. Three series were fired comprised the day on the Rifles Road.	

WAR DIARY or INTELLIGENCE SUMMARY

80th Brigade RFA (1)

Army Form C. 2118

Place	Date 1916	Hour	Summary of Events and Information	Remarks and references to Appendices
VIELLE CHAPELLE	Jan 16		Fire was directed on houses at S.17.a.9.6., S.23.C.9.6. & S.28.A.2.3. Several direct hits were made and enemy retaliation was slight.	
	17		A group scheme was carried out on points B9 line Trenches at S.22.C.3.8. to S.22.C.8.6. Considerable amount was done to the enemy parapets. His retaliation was most intense than has been experienced for some time.	
	18		Climatic conditions for observation has been after 10 a.m.; O.P.'s on the Rue du Bois received attention from the enemy artillery. Principally the LEICESTER LOUNGE and CAFÉ DE L'EUROPE.	
	19		A large portion of Violaines Church disappeared during the afternoon the reason being unknown. Enemy 77 mm guns are very active throughout the day from the direction of the O.15.T.11.10.12.	
	20		Our artillery fired several times during the day at the request of the infantry, and also several instructional series were fired for the 38th Division officers attached to Batteries. Registration was also carried out.	
	21		A machine gun emplacement at S.11.a.4½.3¼ was shelled, 12 direct hits were made - Part of emplacement was blown away and parapet trenches in several places. Enemy retaliated with trench mortars.	

WAR DIARY
or
INTELLIGENCE SUMMARY

86th Brigade RFA
Army Form C. 2118

Place	Date 1916 JAN.	Hour	Summary of Events and Information	Remarks and references to Appendices
NEUVE CHAPELLE	22		There has been little Enemy shelling during the day. Even the bombardment of the Boars Head by the 8" Howitzers to produce retaliation to any degree.	
	23		Lieut. Col. A.E. Wilson DSO Took Command of the Left Artillery Group. vice Lt Col. R.M. Yeomans RFA Evacuated.	
	24	—	Enemy Artillery being inactive during the day, fire was directed on the Enemy front line with considerable effect by the 18 pdrs.	
	25	—	Climatic Conditions were bad all day for observation. 6/1/21 fired 17⁰ 48.+ 7⁰ Shrapnel at the point of the German Salient opposite the Bomb Store. Wire was effectually cut and parapets badly damaged.	
	26		Lieut Col A.E. Wilson DSO. took over Command of the 79th Divisional artillery vice Brig. Gen. R. Fitzhannen on leave. Major H.S. Stratfield RFA Took over Command of the 8th RFA Brigade vice Col Wilson to RA. 19th Divisional RFA	
	27		Enemy artillery paid considerable attention to one O.P.'s on the Rue de Bois, two direct hits being made on the GAIETY.	

86th Brigade RFA (16)

WAR DIARY
or
INTELLIGENCE SUMMARY

Place	Date 1916	Hour	Summary of Events and Information	Remarks and references to Appendices
VIELLE CHAPELLE	JAN 28		A wire cutting scheme was carried out at 5.16. a 4.1/7% observation being made from the front line trench. Some hours of dead branches about and many posts were thrown in the air.	
	29		One section of each battery and ammunition column of the 86th Bde RFA was relieved by the corresponding section of the 119th Brigade RFA, on relief the sections marched to reserve billets west of St Venant.	
	30		The remaining sections and H.Q. 86th Brigade RFA were relieved by 119th Brigade RFA and marched to reserve billets west of St Venant.	
	31		Brigade in reserve billets Estaires	

86th Bde: R.F.a.

19 Vol 6

Army Form C. 2118

WAR DIARY
or
INTELLIGENCE SUMMARY
(Erase heading not required.)

86th Brigade R.F.A. 19th Division

Place	Date 1916	Hour	Summary of Events and Information	Remarks and references to Appendices
ST. VENANT.	1 to 13		Brigade in reserve at St Venant, battery and brigade training	
	14 to 16		Brigade moved into action at NEUVE CHAPELLE relieving the 38th Divisional artillery, forming part of the Right Artillery Group under Colonel A.E. Wilson D.S.O. H.Q. Right Group at M.19.C.4.0. BOUT D'EVILLE	
BOUT DEVILLE.	16		Command of the Right Artillery Group taken over by Colonel A.E. Wilson at 10 a.m.	
	17		Weather conditions for observation bad owing to rain. Enemy artillery quiet.	
	18		Hostile artillery been inactive – Hostile aircraft been busy at night.	
	19		Movements showed great activity on our front line. Suspected position S.I.6.S.2.	
	20	-	Although cloudy light was good for observation – New telephone poles were noticed on Aubers Ridge	

J.J. Johnson LIEUT. R.F.A.
ADJUTANT. 86TH BRIGADE R.F.A.

Army Form C. 2118

(18)

WAR DIARY
or
INTELLIGENCE SUMMARY 86th Brigade R.F.A. 19th Division

(Erase heading not required.)

Place	Date 1916	Hour	Summary of Events and Information	Remarks and references to Appendices
BOUT DEVILLE.	FEB 21		Observation kept at intervals during the day. A light demonstration was carried out by the 18 pdrs and howrs of the Right Group between 10 p.m. and 11.15 p.m. on Houses at S17a Central. The Ov. B162 S12d both the object of driving the enemy from his billets and picking to the open. Batt Sheetwel Fire	
	22		Snow fell heavily, at times making observation difficult motor wheels were noticed on the road running on the East side of Bois d'u B162.	
	23		A combined demonstration took place between the 18 pdrs and Hows in Conjunction with the Heavies on Trenches S11a Central and proved most effective. Enemy retaliated heavily on our front line.	
	24		The combined demonstration was repeated. to 9.I.'s of the 29th Heavy Battery Set the Hun's first round the parapets were breached in 8 places about S.I.G. and 3 large craters were observed. Enemy retaliation was slight	

J. P. Moore LIEUT. R.F.A.
ADJUTANT, 86TH BRIGADE R.F.A.

Army Form C. 2118

WAR DIARY
or
INTELLIGENCE SUMMARY

(Erase heading not required.) 86th Brigade R.F.A. 19th Division

Instructions regarding War Diaries and Intelligence Summaries are contained in F. S. Regs., Part II. and the Staff Manual respectively. Title Pages will be prepared in manuscript.

Place	Date 1916	Hour	Summary of Events and Information	Remarks and references to Appendices
BOUT DEVILLE	FEB 25		Enemy artillery was active from 12.30 p.m to 2.30 p.m. Shrapnel, Whizz bangs and H.E.'s. The vicinity of Plum St, Post, Arthur and Cope Pt were heavily shelled during this time.	
	26		A Combined Strafe took place at 2.30 p.m. 6-bdrs of the 18 pdrs and howrs of the Right Group in Conjunction with the 18 pdrs and 3.3 pdr Trench Mortar Batteries and Stokes Guns at S.10.d.56½. The parapets were destroyed in several places - was very effective. The parapets were destroyed and trenches in several places - and S.10.d.9.9.	
	27		At dawn an artillery Strafe combined with an infantry demonstration took place. Unfortunately the wind was not in the right direction for using Smoke Candles. The Enemy retaliation on our front line and support trenches has been prompt and Effective.	
	28		A torpedo fired by the infantry at S.S.6.9½.9. cut a lane in the wire 6 to 10 yds wide - Enemy artillery was fairly quiet all day.	
	29		The Strafe in Co-operation with the infantry demonstration carried out the Enemy to have his parapets and considerable damage was done to his front line - The Strafe burst well over the trenches from S/36.C.O.9. to S/10.a.O.5.	

G.J. Johnson LIEUT. R.F.A.
ADJUTANT, 86TH BRIGADE R.F.A.

WAR DIARY
or
INTELLIGENCE SUMMARY. 80th Brigade R.F.A.

Army Form C. 2118

Place	Date 1915	Hour	Summary of Events and Information	Remarks and references to Appendices
St VENANT	1 to 13		Brigade in reserve at Pt Venant billets and horses standings	556
	14 to 16		Brigade moved into action at Neuve Chapelle relieving 36th Brigade in Telbar, forming part of the Right Artillery Group under Colonel A.E. Aslam D.S.O.	
	16		Command of the left Artillery Group taken over by Colonel A.E. Aslam at 10 am	
	17		Reserve Contains to observate his moves to our Enemy Artillery Quiet	
	18		Hostile Artillery very inactive — hostile aircraft over lines at night	
	19		Ammunition stores fresh return of our front line inspection position 5 p.m.	
	20		Although Cloudy light was good to observe fire. Enemy's telephone poles and houses on Aubers Ridge	

WAR DIARY or INTELLIGENCE SUMMARY

Army Form C. 2118

86th Brigade R.F.A. 19th Division   457

Place	Date	Hour	Summary of Events and Information	Remarks and references to Appendices
Sept DEVILLE	1916 FEB 21		Observation from O.P. towards Ovillers La Boiselle a high velocity gun was carried out 6 Offrs 18 N.C.Os and Gunners of the Right Group attended. 10 pm S.O.S. started. Guns of BOIS DU BIER Horses at S.27.a twice the enemy put SOS a lilies and railing shell of though the howl fire. Co optn. but short of howl fire.	
	22		Snow fell heavily at times, kept observation difficult wide note where and notices on the Xmas Morning on the East Pits at BOIS DU BIER	
	23		A continued demonstration for places between the 15 pdrs. howtizers in coordination with the Shrines on French S.11.a Central and stones not Shrapnel. 511 enemy returned rounds on our front line.	
	24		The Commander reports registration his reported to 9.Y.: of the 28 Heavy Battery for to new front rounds. The parapet has been in 6 places about S.11.6 and 3 large craters been observed. Lieut.	

WAR DIARY
INTELLIGENCE SUMMARY

(Erase heading not required.)

H.Q. Brigade R.F.A. 19th Division

Place	Date	Hour	Summary of Events and Information	Remarks and references to Appendices
BOIS T DISPUTÉ	25		Enemy artillery was active from 12.30 pm to 2.30 am. She put N.T. ½s and H.E.'s in the vicinity of Plum Pt, Port Arthur and Copse Pt. Men were heavily shelled during the time.	554
	26		A combined attack took place at 2.30 am. One of the 18 pdrs and howrs of the Rifles fought in conjunction but A.P. 15 pdr and 33 pdr times into the Batterys were very effective. The barrage on distance field 55½ and 51.0 d 9.9 was not treated to heavy places.	
	27		At dawn an enemy fast carried out a heavy concentration took place on Battery of A4 in the right direction to many of our batterys on our front line and without back have been sharp at one effective.	
	28		A telephone line by the infantry at S.O.S. No. 2 out came in the beam to 6 to 9.40 pm were taken in which just all day.	
	29		The Frank & Co. Ltd report that the infantry remonstrators are going to try by degrees to take their pupils one to two in the Front Line. The figures however are to testify the fact of...	

19

86 RFA

Vol 7

WAR DIARY or INTELLIGENCE SUMMARY

Army Form C. 2118

Right Group
86 Brigade RFA
XIX to Division

Place	Date 1916 March	Hour	Summary of Events and Information	Remarks and references to Appendices
BOUT DEVILLE	1		Enemy artillery has very active to-day on Neuve Chapelle. Vaugherstogne O.P. practically destroyed. Recommenced by 5 firing. Lieut. Col. Ranneford Hannay took command of the group Sunday afternoon.	20
	2		Arranged for the shelling of Neuve Chapelle between the 9.2's and 2.18pm Batty shells hundred and a house at T1a 1/2, 1/2 which it is thought there were an OPs for the shoot	
	3		A group scheme was carried out on the Neuve Chapelle opposite the het 100 rds at T shell and 1.40 1.8pm 1.2. H.B. were used with good effect	
	4		Weather conditions bad observation difficult and very little firing was done.	
	5		Enemy very quiet all day a few 5.9's fired into Neuve Chapelle about 4 pm and trench bombs on the het at 4-30 pm	
	6		Wire cutting was carried out by B/87 at T.5.d.S.6. 300 rds about effective. Lt Col. S Ranneford Hannay RFA was wounded while observing the fire and Lt Col Deverton RFA took over command of the Right Group.	

Lieut. R.F.A.
Adjutant, 88th Brigade R.F.A.

WAR DIARY or INTELLIGENCE SUMMARY

Army Form C. 2118

Right Group
86th Brigade R.F.A.
XIth Division

(21)

Place	Date	Hour	Summary of Events and Information	Remarks and references to Appendices
BOIS DEVILLE	1916 MARCH 7		Enemy retaliation to an operation by the left group of the 38th Divisional Artillery was prompt and preformed chiefly with 4.2 Hows between Bois St and Factory Corner.	
	8		The house at S.6.b.1½.9 seems to be a tender spot. When ever an by G/89. retaliation on the Chateau Renault Revue Chapelle was almost instantaneous	
	9		The Lap at M.3.5 & 9.3 was considerably damaged by fire from our heavier enemy retaliates at once on Chateau Redoubt and Keep	
	10		The Bois du Biez has had a objective in an organised strafe by the 18pdrs and Hows of the Right Group. The areas was searched from end to end and as far as could be judged good results were obtained	
	11		Enemy artillery was fairly active to-day and each round was repaid by our Batteries	
	12		Lieut Col A.E. Wilson RSO returned from leave and assumed command of the Right Artillery Group.	

J. Stone
LIEUT. R.F.A.
ADJUTANT, 86TH BRIGADE R.F.A.

Army Form C. 2118

WAR DIARY
or
INTELLIGENCE SUMMARY Right Group
8th Brigade R.F.A.
XIXth Division

(Erase heading not required.)

(22)

Place	Date	Hour	Summary of Events and Information	Remarks and references to Appendices
BOUT DEVILLE	1916 MARCH 13.		Enemy artillery of all Calibres was partic- ularly active from 11 o'c onwards. O.P.'s on the Rue du Bois being the main objective. The Boot Factory at Neuve Chapelle was partially destroyed.	
	14		The Enemy continued to work hard on his new afternoon and dark parties can be seen along the Sucre Bois covered by the Fog.	
	15		From 1.25 p.m. to 2.30 p.m. the enemy shelled A/86 position, one man and one horse killed - material damage was trivial.	
	16		Orders were received to limit the expenditure of ammunition to 16 rds per gun	
	17		Enemy artillery has been inactive and our action nil.	
	18		A great deal of air on this front seems working section observed.	
	19		Enemy artillery was inactive although observation balloons were up during the day. Registration by aeroplane was carried out by B/86.	
	20		A time was exploded at the Stoke Box by the Enemy causing a few Casualties. Our front line was supported trenches were heavily shelled afterwards.	

LIEUT. R.F.A.
ADJUTANT, 86TH BRIGADE R.F.A.

WAR DIARY or INTELLIGENCE SUMMARY

Army Form C. 2118

80th Brigade R.F.A.
XIXth Division

23

Place	Date 1916	Hour	Summary of Events and Information	Remarks and references to Appendices
BOUT. DEVILLE	March 21		A systematic bombardment of the Neuve Chapelle area took place between 12.15 pm and 1.30 pm. Shells of all calibres from 8" to 77 m/m's. The north face of the N36 was breached in several places but considering the intensity of the bombardment very little material damage was done. Lacrymatory shells were used by the Germans the fumes of which hung about for several hours. Plum St, Rue St & Copse Street were shelled. Artillery works with all calibres.	
	22	—		
	23	—	Enemy artillery St Trench Quiet and Expenditure by the Regt Group. 19th R.F.A. nil	
	24	—	Snow fell continually until 3 pm having observation impossible. Enemy artillery extremely quiet again.	
	25	—	Enemy artillery has been all day. From 10.15 am to 11.45 am heavy bombardment of our front line - Neuve Chapelle - Mauquissart. At 5 pm an ??? bombarded with our Battalion HQ at the OP's at the north ??? at calibre shells have been in cavity considerable damage of the Rue du Bois & Plum & ???	

GP Moore Lieut. R.F.A.
ADJUTANT 80th BDE

WAR DIARY
or
INTELLIGENCE SUMMARY

Army Form C. 2118

8th Brigade R.F.A.
XIXth Division

Place	Date 1916	Hour	Summary of Events and Information	Remarks and references to Appendices
BOUT DEVILLE	MCH. 26		Enemy artillery quiet to-day and very little firing by Rifles Lidr. The Enemy is hard at work repairing and strengthening his trenches along the entire front.	
	27		Enemy artillery again inactive - many fires were noticed in the new trenches at S.11.d.4.3.	
	28		Several enemy working parties were observed but nothing of particular importance happened.	
	29		Enemy field batteries were active to-day - a direct hit was made on Cavendish House but no damage done to the O.P. post.	
	30		Several Enemy observation balloons were up to-day - there is no doubt the Enemy is taking advantage of our enforced inactivity and reviewing his front.	
	31		An Enemy aeroplane was brought down at Winche Corner S.9.a.6.9/r. Both occupants were killed.	

LIEUT. R.F.A.
ADJUTANT. 86th BRIGADE R.F.A.

Army Form C. 2118

Vol 8 [25]

WAR DIARY
or
INTELLIGENCE SUMMARY
(Erase heading not required.)

86th FA Brigade
XXth Division

Place	Date	Hour	Summary of Events and Information	Remarks and references to Appendices
BOUT DEVILLE	1/6	1	The usual amount of working parties were observed in the enemy lines. At 7.40 p.m. the usual places Crois Barbu Crossroads, under Coun, & Cheton Road with M.G.s.	
		2	Registration by aeroplane was carried out and good results were obtained.	
		3	Enemy artillery was quiet to-day. Subaltr report that the enemy front line appears to be evacuated or held only by sentries during the day. No lifting has previously occurred during the last few days. Enemy are observed in different & may to and from front and second line trenches about S.S.a.5.6.	
		4	About 50 rounds from enemy 5.9 batteries were directed at O.P's on Rue du Bois & round his headqrs on 96 Piccadilly during the evening. Considerable damage	
		5	O.P's on the Rue du Bois were again the chief objective of enemy artillery; the southern end of Streiff down was hit with 8"	

G.P. Ross LIEUT. R.F.A.
ADJUTANT. 86TH BRIGADE R.F.A.

Army Form C. 2118

26

WAR DIARY
or
INTELLIGENCE SUMMARY

86th D.A. Brigade.
XIXth Division

(Erase heading not required.)

Place	Date 1916	Hour	Summary of Events and Information	Remarks and references to Appendices
BOOT DEVILLE	April 7		Enemy artillery has been inactive. A few working parties were noticed, fired on and dispersed.	
	8		The enemy seems to be taking advantage of our enforced inactivity and doing considerable work on his 1st and 2nd lines of trenches.	
	9		A howitzer for enfilement was located, a bare S.W. of S. the gun was observed firing on our trenches right 8/9/R	
	10		Enemy artillery still inactive, one allowance of ammunition was had noth on working parties learned of which were noticed during the day	
	11		Several working parties were notices but nothing of importance happened during the 24 hours.	
	12	-	Light was bad for observation owing to rain and mist.	
	13	-	Several parties of men and horsemen have been during the morning in the vicinity T.25.a.	

J.R. Shore LIEUT. R.F.A.
ADJUTANT. 86TH BRIGADE R.F.A.

Army Form C. 2118

(27)

WAR DIARY
or
INTELLIGENCE SUMMARY

86th FA Brigade
XIXth Division.

(Erase heading not required.)

Place	Date 1916	Hour	Summary of Events and Information	Remarks and references to Appendices
BOUT DEVILLE	April 14		Enemy TM battery was active to-day, Rifle & M.G. fire on our front line trenches. One section of each battery of the Brigade was relieved by the 35th Divisional Artillery and on relief proceeded to rest billets in the St VENANT area.	
	15		The relief of the 86th Brigade RFA by 35th Divisional Artillery was complete at 7 p.m.	
	16 to 21st		Brigade in rest billets at ST VENANT. The usual battery routine being carried out.	
	21st		Brigade moved to 1st Army training area near THEROUANNE being billeted in the village of THEROUANNE	
	22 to 30		Battery and Brigade Training.	

J.D. [signature]
LIEUT. R.F.A.
ADJUTANT, 86th BRIGADE R.F.A.

D.H.G.
   3rd Echelon
      The Base

Herewith War Diary of
86" Brigade R.F.A. for months
of May 1916. and June 1916

                                                        LIEUT: COL: R.F.A.
                                    COMMANDING 86TH BRIGADE R.F.A.

WAR DIARY or INTELLIGENCE SUMMARY

Army Form C. 2118

Vol 8.9
86th Brigade RFA
XIXth Divisional Artillery · May - June 1916

Place	Date	Hour	Summary of Events and Information	Remarks and references to Appendices
THEROUANNE	May 1916 1st to 7th		Training in 1st Army Manoeuvre Area.	
	8th 9th		Brigade moved by batteries to LONGEAU, entraining at LILLERS. From LONGEAU the detraining point batteries moved to billets in YZEUX. The division remaining in GHQ Reserve.	
YZEUX	14th		30 men per battery were sent to the forward area to construct gun pits for occupation later. The 86th FA Brigade is temporarily attached to the 8th Divisional Artillery. Forward Headquarters were established in the town of ALBERT.	
	18th		The Brigade Ammunition Column was broken up the majority of the personnel going to form a new section of the D.A.C.	

J. P. Rowe
LIEUT. R.F.A.
ADJUTANT, 86TH BRIGADE R.F.A.

Army Form C. 2118

86 Brigade R.F.A
XIX Division 29

WAR DIARY
or
INTELLIGENCE SUMMARY
(Erase heading not required.)

Instructions regarding War Diaries and Intelligence Summaries are contained in F. S. Regs., Part II. and the Staff Manual respectively. Title Pages will be prepared in manuscript.

Place	Date	Hour	Summary of Events and Information	Remarks and references to Appendices
YZEUX.	May 25th	—	D/86 Bde R.F.A became A/89th Bde R.F.A (late D/86 R.F.A) A/89 Bde R.F.A became D/86 Bde (late A/89 Bde R.F.A) on reorganization.	
	1st 6th 31st		Remainder of Bde not in forward area carried out Battery training	J Graham Lieut R.F.A

Army Form C. 2118

WAR DIARY
or
INTELLIGENCE SUMMARY
(Erase heading not required.)

Instructions regarding War Diaries and Intelligence Summaries are contained in F. S. Regs., Part II. and the Staff Manual respectively. Title Pages will be prepared in manuscript.

Place	Date June	Hour	Summary of Events and Information	Remarks and references to Appendices
YZEUX	1		Brigade in Divis. on Reserve. Forward H.Q. under 8th Div. M.Q. in ALBERT. Constructing forward gun positions.	
	19		Batteries of the Brigade moved independently to forward positions.	
	22		Brigade complete in forward position in ALBERT	
	24		Brigade H.Q. moved to Dripling Report Centre from ALBERT, and became the Centre group R.A. supporting 25th Inf Bde.	
	25		Batteries register their lines	
	26		C/86 is engaged cutting Enemy's Second Line wire.	
	27		" " " All batteries are given final orders on barrages for next day, when assault takes place. C/86 sustained slight casualties - to their gun pit by heavy fire of 5"9 a direct hit on No 3.	
	~~28~~		Owing to very wet weather the assault was postponed for 48 hours. Sunny	
	28		Shelling very slight. Front line trenches on S. C/86 firing on enemy's line at intervals to prevent repairing.	
	29		Very little shell fire on the front. Centre group material.	
	30		Enemy Shelling front line with all calibres. 9200 Shells 5"9 - 4.2 77mm.	

Signature *(illegible)* LIEUT, R.F.A.
ADJUTANT, 86TH BRIGADE R.F.A.

19th Div.
III.Corps.

WAR DIARY

Headquarters

86th BRIGADE, R.F.A.

JULY

1916

WAR DIARY or INTELLIGENCE SUMMARY

Army Form C.
Vol II

86 RFA

Place	Date	Hour	Summary of Events and Information	Remarks and references to Appendices
ALBERT	1916 July 1	7.30 a.m.	At 7.30 a.m. the general offensive was opened on the Corps front. The Corps front comprising 86th Brigade and A/89 bombards the enemy's 3rd line trenches across the Tropoved and lifts its shells as laid down in the programme the 8th Div Arty. Is the CRIMSON or last line defended by POZIERES.	
		10.30 a.m.	At the Artie front, 18 pdrs were turned into a barrage of shrapnel sweeping to the SE at the left boundary of the 8th Div. The Howitzer battery sweeping St THIEPVAL on the left boundary of the enemy's strong point. The trenches on the left of the 8th Div' area SE of THIEPVAL and trenches at communication trench in this area, the	
			4.5 How battery sweeping strong points shortly the M.A.B. The group sweeps through the trenches to the right of the 8th Div' zone is the rear of OVILLERS LA BOISELLE. Hours of sweeping strong point in OVILLERS LA BOISELLE. In the morning of a direct hit was made on No. 4 gun after 4–5 Hrs batting – a 5.9 shell exactly hit the gun much of the pit completely damaging the gun and putting only if action the whole of the 6 gun detachment – a 5.9 shell struck the left of No. 2 pit. the band battery but no damage was done.	
			Groups were employed in searching communication trenches between OVILLERS LA BOISELLE and POZIERES. The battery was in continuous action for 72 hours and fired about 27000 rounds of ammunition.	
		5.30 p.m.	The Brigade less A/89 withdrew from the mop line and tough to DER NANCOURT, and came under the orders of the 19th Div' Arty. A/89 remains to it own Brigade. The casualties during this period	

WAR DIARY or INTELLIGENCE SUMMARY

Army Form C. 2118

Place	Date	Hour	Summary of Events and Information	Remarks and references to Appendices
ALBERT	1916 July 7		In action amounted to 2 killed and 16 wounded.	
	7		New groups formed unit B/88 in action covering CONTALMAISON at X 27 a 6.7 and was the most forward position of the Division. B/88 in action against trenches on the right of 7th D/86 D/A/86 move into a position close to ALBERT and just south of it.	
	8		Brig. Bailey position near reconnoitred to the locat of PRICOURT. D/86 (How) D/A/86 & B pr to Contn CONTALMAISON and POZIERES. Three batteries move into their present pos. on night of 8th/9th Brigade H.Q. established in BECOURT WOOD. Batteries opened fire and register Zero hour.	
	9 10		At 3 p.m. batteries opened fire on approaches to POZIERES, at 4.20 p.m. batteries opened fire and advance on CONTALMAISON at 5.50 p.m. CONTALMAISON taken with 190 prisoners. at 9.55 p.m. opened barrage on counter attack.	
	11		B/88 sent forward a gun to CONTALMAISON to cut wire to the south POZIERES. The forward gun was hurriedly dug in showing a counter attack by the enemy — GN 5.30 p.m. Capt. McLEOD & Dpl. & Lt. CUDMORE D/A/86 were wounded —	
		4 p.m	B/88 was relieved by B/86 — B/88 — C/86 Came into action taking our D/A/86 position. B/88 advancing their battery to the S.E. Corner of BAILIFF WOOD. B/86 taking our C/86 forward gun in CONTALMAISON.	
	13 14 15 16		Brigade was subjected to continuing the assaults on POZIERES.	
	17		Brigade H.Q. move into dugouts in German 3rd line trench 500 yards South of OVILLERS LA BOISELLE	

WAR DIARY or INTELLIGENCE SUMMARY

Army Form C. 2118

Place	Date 1916	Hour	Summary of Events and Information	Remarks and references to Appendices
ALBERT	18th		Bombardment of POZIERES which continued prior to assault by Infantry.	
	19th	9 am	The howitzer batty using THERMITE softened div. Artillery. Bde. was not very satisfactory. Bde Brigade was relieved by 1st Australian Div. Artillery and moved into action in a position 1 MILE NORTH of MARTINPUICH coming MARTINPUICH. Batteries withdrawing zone the same day.	
	20th			
	21st		During this period the Bdy. batteries were subjected to heavy enemy shell fire of every calibre - usually in heavy concentration to the dusk. Batteries including Lt.Col. A.E. Major S.T. MILSON. D.S.O. wounded	Major S.T. Hay taken Command
	22nd		on the Bgde HQ. moved to a position 200 yards north of Fabian afr.	
	23rd		CATAPILLAR WOOD. The Command of the Brigade being taken over by MAJOR COOKE R.F.A. On the night of 24th Batteries moved into new positions 500 yards South of CATAPILLAR WOOD. Brigade HQ. being established 100 yards South	
	24th		of battery position.	
	25th		Batteries withdrew their zones.	
	26th		On night of 26 & 27th batteries moved into new positions. A/86 occupying a position 300 yards N.W. of MARLBRO' WOOD. B/86 & C/86 occupying positions 300 yards South of BAZENTIN LE PETIT WOOD. Brigade HQ. established 200 yards N.W. of MARLBORO WOOD.	Major Cooke going Sick Major S.T. HAY again Take Comd.
	27th		Batteries within their Zones on SWITCH LINE & INTERMEDIATE TRENCHES.	
	28th			
	29th			
	30th			
	31st		Batteries co-operated with Infantry for assault on INTERMEDIATE LINE & HIGH WOOD	

Army Form C. 2118

(4)

WAR DIARY
or
INTELLIGENCE SUMMARY

(Erase heading not required.)

Place	Date	Hour	Summary of Events and Information	Remarks and references to Appendices
ALBERT	20 Feb 31st		The total casualties to the Brigade during this period amounts to eight Officers and fourteen other ranks. R.L. Lean Major Commanding 86th T.M. Bde.	

19th Divisional Artillery.

86th BRIGADE

ROYAL FIELD ARTILLERY

AUGUST 1 9 1 6 :::::

WAR DIARY or INTELLIGENCE SUMMARY

Army Form C. 2118

Vol 12

Place: ALBERT
Date: AUGUST 1916

Date	Hour	Summary of Events and Information	Remarks and references to Appendices
1.		During the 2 guns of A/86 being out of action the battery Zone were re-allotted as follows :— SWITCH LINE. C/86 S.36.d.9.7. — M.33.d.0.0. B/86. M.33.d.0.0 — M.33.c.3.2. A/86. M.33.C.3.2. — M.33.C.2.0. — Order received that 19th Div Arty would be relieving us. 15th Div arty on night of 3rd/4th. Major E.S. Hay Commanding 15th Div Arty came over to hospital — Major Cox of C/89 being probs to the Brigade to take command.	
2.	10am		
	9.30am 1.30pm	Enemy kept up a slow rate of fire with Sig" & 8" on CATERPILLAR WOOD VALLEY — hostile planes active all day. 19th Inf Bde arriving at the approved of infantry we carried out a small programme on the INTERMEDIATE LINE—	
3.	8pm 5pm	Arty of both sides very active all day. CATERPILLAR WOOD & VALLEY SWITCH LINE was bombarded for 30 mins	
4 night 3/4		One section of each battery was relieved by one section by 13th FA Bde. 15th Div Arty the relieving section marching into the night to Batter, major line. guns were handed over in battery positions — relieving guns came on at In battery to BEHENCOURT.	
4	7.30am	The relieving section marched individually to BEHENCOURT AREA taking on the battery mix of 73rd FA Bde. in camp. O.P.s handed over—	
night 4/5		Relieving battery commanders shown round O.P.s handed over — The remainder of 73rd FA Bde relieve the remainder of 86th Bde. Relief being complete at 4am. 5th Command of Group handed over to O.C. 13th Bde — Brigade H.Q. + remaining sections of 86th Brigade marching to BEHERN COURT via old major mine.	
5	8.15pm	Brigade marches to BAVELINCOURT and encamped.	
6	10am	Brigade marches to LONGUEAU under by GENERAL BIRCHAM in camp.	
		Brigade entraining at LONGUEAU to entrain in the following order	
		A/86 at 9.13 pm 6.8.16	
		B/86 do 12.18 am 7.8.16	
		C/86 do 3.28 am 7.8.16	
		D/86 do 6.13 am 7.8.16	
		H.Q. do 8.46 am 7.8.16	
7		At same being duty of Adjutant + 2nd Divn Adj. D/Arden	

1875. Wt. W 593/826 1,000,000 4/15 J.B.C. & A. A.D.S.S./Forms/C.2118.
Lt F.W. Marshall took Command of C/86

WAR DIARY or INTELLIGENCE SUMMARY

Army Form C. 2118

86 A.B.92

Place	Date	Hour	Summary of Events and Information	Remarks and references to Appendices
	7		The quarters of the D.A.C. entraining with each battery. Batteries detrained at CASSEL and marched to billets at STEENVOORDE. Headquarters detrained at STEENVOORDE joining battery at STEENVOORDE. Brigade remained night in billets —	
	night 7/8 8		Brigade H.Q. & Batteries marched independently during afternoon to DRANOUTRE to relieve 252 Brigade R.F.A. A/86 relieving A/252 at wagon lines N.b. i. 8.6 — A/86 not being in action because the reserve battery. Relief by sections of B.C. & D/252 by sections of B.C. & D/86. Guns were not exchanged —	
	night 8/9 & 9/10		Command of Brigade assumed at 12 noon 9 — B.C. D/86 confirmed the RIGHT GROUP. Covering 57th Infantry Brigade. Registration of zones by batteries —	
	10 & night 10/11		The front covered by Brigade was considered too large to be protected by 2 18 pdr batteries and no 4.5" How — Arrangements A/86 two troops out of reserve B. & D batteries being from north to south – B/86 - C/86. A/86 – 7/19 R.F.H. attached to Right Group.	
	11		Registration completed – O.P.'s for A.C. & D/86 arranged for KEMMEL HILL. Mutual Support Scheme with 36th Division and Batteries astride - which	
	12 13 14		are now from North to South B/86. A/86 – C/86 – Scheme for Co-ordination with Aeroplanes & wires — two large spaces in map being given to each. 18 prs batting.	
	15"	3.30pm	A bombardment in conjunction with shrapnel Heavies carried out on enemy front & Support lines — Right Group were not inclined to believe that Lord Kitchener's take away advantage of targets which presented themselves and to open rapid bursts should the enemy prevent themselves retaliated.	

WAR DIARY or INTELLIGENCE SUMMARY

Army Form C. 2118

Place	Date	Hour	Summary of Events and Information	Remarks and references to Appendices
DRANOUTRE	14		Trench retaliation scheme arranged - Trench a code range now fixed to each section of our front line- Enemy kind of [illegible] scheme for retaliation-	
	16	3.30pm	Bombarded by H.T.M. & Enemy front surface line - Repro Group Co-operating. 4T.M's was mounted & 38 bombs at N.90; 1 French mortar school the division. The bombardment lasting about an hour - 2) bombs being fires - they being retaliation in the enemy.	
	17		Enemy active - T.M.'s fairly active all day on front & front line top & to country mainly it almost impossible to locate T.M. Batteries. On observation with 6" Howitzers he been of Right front being to engage any suspected enemy OPs & retaliate where it the occurs. Got line two rifle grenade advisory no movement being observed when trains came on the front say -	
	18			
	19			
	20			
	21	3.30pm	W/19. T.M.B. bombarded enemy front line - Repro front co-operating by retaliating communication trenches.	
	22		Enemy T.M fire seems to be decreasing since the Division took over. it meant front - practically no TM fire -	
	23			
	24	3.30pm	W/19 & 2/19. T.M.B. bombarded front line trench on Repro Group front- Repro front retaliating communication trenches as every few- 6" Howitzer also co-operating- chaining f line + retaliation-	
	25			
	26	11.9pm 1.46pm	Bombardment lasting f hour - had him as a relief in laying places in laying information	

Army Form C. 2118

WAR DIARY
or
INTELLIGENCE SUMMARY
(Erase heading not required.)

B.W.

Place	Date	Hour	Summary of Events and Information	Remarks and references to Appendices
BRAQUIRE	29/30/31	23p.m	2/19 Iron B. cut wire on every front line — the rifle fire on/o firing covering fire on each occasion	

M.H.O.
Major R.M.
On/p 86th Brigade R.M.

Vol 13

CONFIDENTIAL

War Diary
of
86th Brigade, R.G.A.
from 1.9.16 to 30.9.16

(Volume XV)

Army Form C. 2118

WAR DIARY or INTELLIGENCE SUMMARY

(Erase heading not required.)

Instructions regarding War Diaries and Intelligence Summaries are contained in F.S. Regs., Part II. and the Staff Manual respectively. Title Pages will be prepared in manuscript.

Appendix XV

Place	Date	Hour	Summary of Events and Information	Remarks and references to Appendices
AYMOUTH	SEPTEMBER 1.		Preparations were made for a minor offensive - but weather intervened and scheme was abandoned. Scheme again abandoned, owing to weather conditions.	
	2. 3. 4.	10 a.m.	14th Divisional Artillery taking over the front of 23rd Divisional Artillery. Lt. Front [illegible] for the time being as Rehabilitation of [illegible] have been [illegible]. The Right Group consisting under Command of Q.O.C. 36 Div Arty & becoming Left Group by Aug.	
	5.	10 p.m.	Scheme originally intended to be carried out between 1st & 13th was cancelled but without the gun. Shell sufficing the [illegible] silently – the shoot through was carried out by gun & [illegible] later – he ordered [illegible] firing [illegible] to be known within in the front line – the fuse was [illegible] bursting in the enemy wire 20 yards after the [illegible] was given.	
	6.	4 p.m.	A bombardment of the enemy front line opposite the St. Eloi front was carried out by all batteries – all [illegible] night firing took place on several suspected	
	7.		Relief of 19th D.A. by [illegible] hq 36 F.D.A. one half of B/86 was relieved by ½ B/154 – One half C/86 by C/150. The relieving sections not ready to mount weapons were to mount upon their line.	
			D/86 relieved by ½ D/173. The relieving sections of D/86 going into action in D/173's do positions. Relief carried out in daylight. C/86 completed by 5/154 – the above relief of ½ & ½ found D/86 completed out by being relieved – guns in each case hauled over in position – D/86 now in action as a battery in D/173's position. A/86 intend to 1st weapons were intact 15th weapon line completed – D/86	
	9.	1 noon	The re-organisation of the Boxy advance is B/86 has was completed – C/86 was known up. – the W-section [illegible] is B/86 & the right is BA/86. – Lt J.W.T. NEWBERY having been commander A/87. He left as commander now as above. – A/86 commanded by Major. P.J.B. HEELAS (2nd Lt [illegible])- B/86. Captain A.S. PETERSON. D.S.O. D/86. Lt H.F. STEPHEN'S (2nd Lt [illegible])	

1875 Wt. W593/826 1,000,000 4/15 J.B.C. & A. A.D.S.S./Forms/C. 2118.

WAR DIARY or INTELLIGENCE SUMMARY

Army Form C. 2118

Place	Date	Hour	Summary of Events and Information	Remarks and references to Appendices
PLOEGSTEERT	9/10		Two sections of A/86 relieve two sections B/173 one section C/173	
	10/11		One section A/86 completes relief of B/173 - also B/86 completes relief of C/173. The two 18 pdr batteries now living in action under O.C. 73 Bde - B/173. C/173 & D/173 being withdrawn.	
NEUVE EGLISE II	11		At 11 a.m. the command of 86 DAC & Brigade passes to Colonel F.R. HANNAY leaving over command of 86 DAC. Major G.H.F. Cox who went to Amiens A/88. Lt. H.F. STEPHENS joins the Brigade and takes over command of D/86 - Registration of new zones - 2nd Lt. P.S. being on H.L. 63.	
	12			
	13		on 13th Major P.J.B. HEELAS joins his Brigade from Hospital to command A/86.	
	14		Wire was cut on enemy front line system by A & B Btys - both having 2 guns in an advanced position to the purpose - D/86 registers hostile enemy front by night 14/15 A & B Btys which drive in supper 15 batteries positions - he remains quiet all day up in advances positions to deal with enemy wire cutting parties by A & B batteries -	
	15	15/16	heavy enfilading coming out to his retaliation of 67th Infantry Brigade - the 67th Infantry Co. operating according to programme - which lasted 12 min.	
	16/17		Accident with an N.C.O. & filler shell in B/86 - the truck zig zag and rocket lying blown out - 3 killed & 3 wounded including 2nd Lt. A.R. ROBINSON -	
	17		D/86 changed her position particulars with be forwarded	
	18			

Army Form C. 2118

WAR DIARY
or
INTELLIGENCE SUMMARY

(Erase heading not required.)

Instructions regarding War Diaries and Intelligence Summaries are contained in F.S. Regs., Part II and the Staff Manual respectively. Title Pages will be prepared in manuscript.

Place	Date	Hour	Summary of Events and Information	Remarks and references to Appendices
NEUVE EGLISE	19		Nothing particular occurred.	
	20		Only a few rounds fired. Hostile artillery very quiet.	
	21	12.40pm	Hostile Balloon brought down in flames by one of our aeroplanes. The Thos Balloon which was up at the same time immediately descended.	
	22		Hostile artillery now active vicinity of Hill 63 shelled.	
	23		Slight hostile artillery activity. Observation difficult in morning because of mist.	
	24	7pm	B/6 observed a working party at V.2.d.5.3.	
	25	6.20pm	One of our aeroplanes called us up and we fired on Schutzgt tram. No hostile artillery fire.	
	26		B.O. met and front line trenches 2nd Birmingham was attached to the Brigade.	
	27	2.30pm	Sgt Dooley, B/6 was presented with Medal by Lt Genl L. Gough. 2 slaves and Spl. Williams with Military Medal by Stanley bombardier near Bomb Villages for gallantry in the former.	
	28		0 Factorio order was sent out to Battern. No further enemy action in the forthcoming scheme in the evening two guns 13/16 moved to wire cutting position at V.20.a.9.7. One gun from A/16 and D/16 totals of infilade positions. D/16 registered then flash gun.	
	29		B/16 but two teams in every gun.	
	30	10p.	In connection with a raid by the Infantry on a German Battery post, the Brigade supplied covering fire. No prisoners were taken, the working party returned safely, and we then shook up fire in concentrations A.	

J. Rainton Hannay
Lt Col
Comd 88 Bde RFA

1875 Wt. W593/826 1,000,000 4/15 J.B.C. & A. A.D.S.S./Forms/C. 2118.

Vol 14

WAR DIARY
OF
86th BDE. R.F.A.
for 1st Oct. to 31st. Oct. 1916

Army Form C. 2118

WAR DIARY
or
INTELLIGENCE SUMMARY

(Erase heading not required.)

86th T. F. A. Brigade. (42)

Place	Date	Hour	Summary of Events and Information	Remarks and references to Appendices
NEUVE EGLISE	OCTOBER 1		Half Batteries of the 14 Bde. R.H.A. relieved half Batteries of 86 Bde. The relief being so fellows, "F" and "T" Batteries R.H.A. relieved A and B Batteries 86 Bde. D/14 relieved D/86. Outgoing half Batteries marched to billets.	
	2		Remaining half Batteries now relieved as above and marched to take billets at Meteren. Brigade Hqrs. moved to Bailleul billets in the afternoon.	
METEREN	3		Guns were examined and those taken over from 14 Bde. R.H.A. were found to be in bad condition.	
FLETRE	4			
	5		Entrained dept. Godewaersvelde at 9 am, detrained at Candas about 3 p.m.	
VAUCHELLES	6		O.C. went up to front with B.O.C. M.T.	
	7		O.C. and Battery Commanders went to Hebuterne to reconnoitre positions. Brigade moved STOIGNEUX.	
	8		Batteries went up to positions and commenced work on them.	
COIGNEUX	9		Brigade Headquarters moved up to HEBUTERNE.	
HEBUTERNE	10		Batteries working hard on positions in HEBUTERNE. Villages quiet frequently shelled and machine guns played on it at night.	
	11			
	12		A and B Batteries commenced digging new cutting positions.	
	13		Positions in HEBUTERNE abandoned and guns brought into action at night in new cutting positions.	
	14		Batteries registered from new cutting positions.	
	15		Brigade Headquarters moved from HEBUTERNE to a tank in vicinity of new cutting positions.	
	16		Whole Brigade withdrew from action and came back to wagon lines.	
	17		Brigade marched to new wagon lines between Albert and Fricourt. U.B. and B.B.C. met in above country to reconnoitre positions near Mangret Farm. Batteries came up into action about midnight and early next morning. Roads in very bad condition due to rain and Batteries could not get their guns right up to their positions.	

1875 Wt. W593/826 1,000,000 4/15 J.B.C. & A. A.D.S.S./Forms/C. 2118.

Army Form C. 2118

WAR DIARY
or
INTELLIGENCE SUMMARY

88th F.A. Brigade

(43)

(Erase heading not required.)

Instructions regarding War Diaries and Intelligence Summaries are contained in F. S. Regs., Part II. and the Staff Manual respectively. Title Pages will be prepared in manuscript.

Place	Date (OCTOBER)	Hour	Summary of Events and Information	Remarks and references to Appendices
ALBERT	18		Brigade Headquarters moved up to position just behind Battery. Battery registered during morning.	
	19		Battery completed registration by noon. Operations postponed for two days.	
	20		Registration verified.	
	21	2.7 p.	At this hour an attack was made on Regina Trench which was entirely successful. Between 600 and 700 prisoners taken on our front. Enemy barrage was very light. Casualties: Killed nil. Wounded Capt H.F. STEPHENS D/86 and 5 O.R.	
	22		Enemy defences not approached. Fired on by day and night.	
	23		Intense bombardment for 15 minutes. Total falls at 6 a.m. New Zone allotted to Bde. OP's difficult to obtain. Lines always breaking	
	24		Registration of new Zone. Regina Trench bombarded from 6–6.15 am again took place	
	25		Registration carried on by Battery. OP. difficult to find at the	
	26	5.32 am	High ground round STUFF REDOUBT very much shelled. Heavy bombardment from 6am – 6.15 am on open ground. No new SOS sent up on our front. No was maintained for ten minutes. Heavy bombardment from 6 – 6.15 am again carried out. Enemy defences kept under fire.	
	27		Registration continued. Enemy defences kept under fire.	
	28	11.30 a	Enemy bombarded STUFF TRENCH for about half an hour. Enemy defences kept under fire by Hostile Battery located at L.34.d.8.5.	
	29	4.15 p	Placed Howitzer guns in action, fired 30 rounds.	
	30		OP line being continually cut by shell fire. Kept enemy defences under trench fire.	
	31	3.45 & 4.30 p	HESSIAN and FITZPATRICK TRENCHES heavily shelled. Enemy defences and new trenches kept under trench fire.	

F.R. Stoveney
Lt. Col.
Cmdg. 88" B. de R.F.A.

Army Form C. 2118

86th F.A Brigade

Sept 15 (44)

WAR DIARY or INTELLIGENCE SUMMARY
(Erase heading not required.)

Place	Date NOVEMBER 1916	Hour	Summary of Events and Information	Remarks and references to Appendices
ALBERT.	1.		Wind on enemy defences and near trenches during the 24 hours. O.P. J A/86	
	2.		Hostile shelled.	
	3.		Fifth enemy defences under hostile fire.	
	4.		Hostile enemy defences under bursts of fire both day and night.	
	5.		Fired on enemy line intermittently throughout the day & night.	
	6.		Two of the enemy front line garrisons were seen walking towards MIRAUMONT. A hostile battery which was observed firing was fired on by the Reserve Brigade. During the morning many waggons were seen on the MIRAUMONT-ACHIET LE PETIT ROAD but unfortunately the wire to the battery was broken at the time. Another hostile battery was engaged while the bridges over the ANCRE & dug outs in the zone were engaged. Aeroplanes run the ANCRE & enemy's defences kept under fire all day.	
	7.			
	8.		Enemy gun flashes were seen during the morning. In the afternoon much traffic was seen on the MIRAUMONT-ACHIET-LE-PETIT ROAD. During the day D/86 registered a shell hit on a BOCHE O.P. The enemy shelled STUFF REDOUBT & HESSIAN TRENCH all day and he also shelled and batteries near MOUQUET FARM.	
	9.	11.30	An enemy Red Cross waggon which was not fired on by us was seen going from GRANDCOURT to MIRAUMONT ONT & in the afternoon 2 trains were seen proceeding in the direction of PUISIEUX-au-MONT. Enemy's defences kept under fire all day & various aeroplane calls were complied with. No hostile fire on our own trenches to-day. C/186 ambushed for trains.	
	10.	1.15 pm	Two enemy aeroplanes flew very low over ZOLLERN and HESSIAN Trenches. At dawn we carried out an intense bombardment of their front line. He retaliated fairly heavily. During the afternoon over 50 4.2 hav. shells fell near STUFF REDOUBT.	
	11.		D/86 fired into GRANDCOURT; the Howitzer shot not five all day.	
	12.		Movement was to be seen on the BEAUCOURT-MIRAUMONT road and morning traffic were seen. Enemy's defences were kept under fire. FIELD TRENCH is most impassable. The new battery C/186 joined to-day.	
	13.		Registration on an attack on the BEAUMONT HAMEL - BEAUCOURT Attack on and after entirely successful	
	14.		Early this morning OC B/86 wounded by machine gun bullet. A rolling barrage was carried out this morning. Batteries are now firing in DESIRE TRENCH, LUCKY WAY & BOIS d'HOLLANDE. Enemy shelled out front line heavily all morning.	

1875. Wt. W593/826 1,000,000 4/15 J.B.C. & A. A.D.S.S./Forms/C. 2118.

WAR DIARY
or
INTELLIGENCE SUMMARY
(Erase heading not required.)

Army Form C. 2118

Instructions regarding War Diaries and Intelligence Summaries are contained in F.S. Regs., Part II. and the Staff Manual respectively. Title Pages will be prepared in manuscript.

Place	Date	Hour	Summary of Events and Information	Remarks and references to Appendices
Nr ALBERT	NOVEMBER 15th		All trenches in The Zone were kept under fire and as far as ammunition would allow Zone calls were answered. D/46 engaged a machine gun in the evening on green rockets were observed on the Zone. Batteries immediately opened fire on the S.O.S. lines. Soon afterwards the liaison officers reported that heavy shelling of our trenches was dying down.	
	16.		About 6 a.m. the front became quiet again. A distinct smell of gas was detected about 6.20 p.m. D/46 fired on any activity in the zone while the 18pdrs shelled front line & back areas. Enemy artillery was very quiet.	
	17		A very quiet day. D/86 engaged a machine gun in support line.	
	18.		Attack on GRAND COURT carried out that was not initially successful. Another barrage was put up in the evening at 5 p.m. but the infantry did not attack. A body of the enemy seen moving E of GRAND COURT were shelled and dispersed. Situation in	
	19.		F.O.D. reports that parties of N. troops can be seen in O.C.2. During the day enemy shelled junction 70.0.1.5. LUCKY WAY	
	20.		Parties of enemy men seen during the morning working on the new trenches leading S. from MIRAUMONT. But men were seen in LUCKY WAY. One of our aeroplanes was brought down at 8.45 a.m. Enemy observed a direct hit on one of our stranded Tanks near STUFF.	
	21	4.45 pm	Trenches fired a heavy bombardment on enemy front line trenches at 5 p.m. All was quiet again in STRABOLGI and in intense bombardment From 6.10 to 5.15. Very quiet all day.	
	22.			
	23.	4.15 pm	Organized bombardment of enemy defences. Retaliation light & very poor all day. Organized bombardment of enemy defences carried out at 4.15.	
	24.		Rain & Mist prevented observation all day. Enemy lines kept under fire during day & night.	
	25		Rain & Mist again all day. Prisoner captured today interrogated by our Liaison officer.	
	26		Usual Day & Night programme carried out.	
	27.			
	28.		Misty all day. Fired 350 gas shells into the QUARRY in MIRAUMONT.	

Army Form C. 2118

WAR DIARY
or
INTELLIGENCE SUMMARY
(Erase heading not required.)

Instructions regarding War Diaries and Intelligence Summaries are contained in F. S. Regs., Part II. and the Staff Manual respectively. Title Pages will be prepared in manuscript.

Place	Date	Hour	Summary of Events and Information	Remarks and references to Appendices
Nr ALBERT	Novr 29.	5.40pm	Mist again made observation impossible. Retaliate with Stokes fires on PUISIEUX & RIVER TRENCHES.	
	30.	5.35am	Retaliation on Enemy lines for shelling our front line trenches. Enemy 18 pdrs on Ext trenches throughout the day. 2 Lt J.W. Rae posted to command B/81. Capt H. Peterson D.S.O.	

F.D. Harvey.
LIEUT. COL. R.F.A.
COMMANDING 65th BRIGADE R.F.A.

WAR DIARY
or
INTELLIGENCE SUMMARY
(Erase heading not required.)

86 Bde R7A Army Form C. 2118

December 1916

Place	Date	Hour	Summary of Events and Information	Remarks and references to Appendices
Nr ALBERT.	1.		Mostly all day observation unfavorable. Programme Carried out during 11-30 - 12-0 Noon. K DEPTS COY B/86 Killed at Battery Position. 442 Bursts near Bing Oak piece entered head + penetrated the Brain.	
	2.		Misty again all day. Enemy defences kept under fire throughout the day + night. Enemy quieter.	
	3.		Enemy defences kept under fire throughout the day + night.	
	4.		Withdrew from Action to Wagon Line at ALBERT.	
	5.		Marched to Rest Billet at AUTHIEULE.	
	8.		Bde marched to new billets as follows:- Hd Qrs + A/86. OCCOCHES B/86 FROHEN-LE-PETIT. C+D/86 MEZEROLLES	
	10.		Bde Hd Qrs moved to FROHEN-LE-PETIT.	
	18.		Inspection of Bde by Major General Commanding 5th Corps near MEZEROLLES. (Marching Order).	
	19. 20.		Party of 1 N.C.O. and to Men per Battery left to prepare positions for the Bde to come into action near HEBUTERNE	

J.R. Henning.
LIEUT: COL: R.F.A.
COMMANDING 86TH BRIGADE R.F.A.

www.ingramcontent.com/pod-product-compliance
Lightning Source LLC
Chambersburg PA
CBHW081448160426
43193CB00013B/2410